THE WATKINSON EVENING

Eliza Leslie

[ZHINGOORA BOOKS]

Mrs. Morland, a polished and accomplished woman, was the widow of a distinguished senator from one of the western states, of which, also, her husband had twice filled the office of governor. Her daughter having completed her education at the best boarding-school in Philadelphia, and her son being about to graduate at Princeton, the mother had planned with her children a tour to Niagara and the lakes, returning by way of Boston. On leaving Philadelphia, Mrs. Morland and the delighted Caroline stopped at Princeton to be present at the annual commencement, and had the happiness of seeing their beloved Edward receive his diploma as bachelor of arts; after hearing him deliver, with great applause, an oration on the beauties of the American character. College youths are very prone to treat on subjects that imply great experience of the world. But Edward Morland was full of kind feeling for everything and everybody; and his views of life had hitherto been tinted with a perpetual rose-color.

Mrs. Morland, not depending altogether upon the celebrity of her late husband, and wishing that her children should see specimens of the best society in

3

the northern cities, had left home with numerous letters of introduction. But when they arrived at New York, she found to her great regret, that having unpacked and taken out her small traveling desk, during her short stay in Philadelphia, she had strangely left it behind in the closet of her room at the hotel. In this desk were deposited all her letters, except two which had been offered to her by friends in Philadelphia. The young people, impatient to see the wonders of Niagara, had entreated her to stay but a day or two in the city of New York, and thought these two letters would be quite sufficient for the present. In the meantime she wrote back to the hotel, requesting that the missing desk should be forwarded to New York as soon as possible.

On the morning after their arrival at the great commercial metropolis of America, the Morland family took a carriage to ride round through the principal parts of the city, and to deliver their two letters at the houses to which they were addressed, and which were both situated in the region that lies between the upper part of Broadway and the North River. In one of the most fashionable streets they found the elegant mansion of Mrs. St. Leonard; but on stopping at the door, were informed that its mistress was not at home. They then left the introductory letter (which they had prepared for this mischance, by enclosing it in an envelope with a card), and proceeding to another street considerably farther up, they arrived at the dwelling of the Watkinson family, to the mistress of which the other Philadelphia letter was directed. It was one of a large block of houses all exactly alike, and all shut up from top to bottom, according to a custom more prevalent in New York than in any other city.

Here they were also unsuccessful; the servant who came to the door telling them that the ladies were particularly engaged and could see no company. So they left their second letter and card and drove off, continuing their ride till they reached the Croton water works, which they quitted the carriage to see and admire. On returning to the hotel, with the intention after an hour or two of rest to go out again, and walk till near dinner-time, they found waiting them a note from Mrs. Watkinson, expressing her regret that she had not been able to see them when they called; and explaining that her family duties always obliged her to deny herself the pleasure of receiving morning visitors, and that her servants had general orders to that effect. But she requested their company for that evening (naming nine o'clock as the hour), and particularly desired an immediate answer.

"I suppose," said Mrs. Morland, "she intends asking some of her friends to meet us, in case we accept the invitation; and therefore is naturally desirous of a reply as soon as possible. Of course we will not keep her in suspense. Mrs. Denham, who volunteered the letter, assured me that Mrs. Watkinson was one of the most estimable women in New York, and a pattern to the circle in which she moved. It seems that Mr. Denham and Mr. Watkinson are connected in business. Shall we go?"

The young people assented, saying they had no doubt of passing a pleasant evening.

The billet of acceptance having been written, it was sent off immediately, entrusted to one of the errand-goers belonging to the hotel, that it might be received in advance of the next hour for the dispatch-post—and Edward Morland desired the man to get into an omnibus with the note that no time might be lost in delivering it. "It is but right"—said he to his mother—"that we should give Mrs. Watkinson an ample opportunity of making her preparations, and sending round to invite her friends."

"How considerate you are, dear Edward"—said Caroline—"always so thoughtful of every one's convenience. Your college friends must have idolized you."

"No"—said Edward—"they called me a prig." Just then a remarkably handsome carriage drove up to the private door of the hotel. From it alighted a very elegant woman, who in a few moments was ushered into the drawing-room by the head waiter, and on his designating Mrs. Morland's family, she advanced and gracefully announced herself as Mrs. St. Leonard. This was the lady at whose house they had left the first letter of introduction. She expressed regret at not having been at home when they called; but said that on finding their letter, she had immediately come down to see them, and to engage them for the evening. "Tonight"—said Mrs. St. Leonard—"I expect as many friends as I can collect for a summer party. The occasion is the recent marriage of my niece, who with her husband has just returned from their bridal excursion, and they will be soon on their way to their residence in Baltimore. I think I can promise you an agreeable evening, as I expect some very delightful people, with whom I shall be most happy to make you acquainted."

Edward and Caroline exchanged glances, and could not refrain from looking wistfully at their mother, on whose countenance a shade of regret was very apparent. After a short pause she replied to Mrs. St. Leonard—"I am truly sorry to say that we have just answered in the affirmative a previous invitation for this very evening."

"I am indeed disappointed"—said Mrs. St. Leonard, who had been looking approvingly at the prepossessing appearance of the two young people. "Is there no way in which you can revoke your compliance with this unfortunate first invitation—at least, I am sure, it is unfortunate for me. What a vexatious *contretemps* that I should have chanced to be out when you called; thus missing the pleasure of seeing you at once, and securing that of your society for this evening? The truth is, I was disappointed in some of the preparations that had been sent home this morning, and I had to go myself and have the things rectified, and was detained away longer than I expected. May I ask to whom you are engaged this evening? Perhaps I know the lady—if so, I should be very much tempted to go and beg you from her."

"The lady is Mrs. John Watkinson"—replied Mrs. Morland—"most probably she will invite some of her friends to meet us."

"That of course"—answered Mrs. St. Leonard—"I am really very sorry—and I regret to say that I do not know her at all."

"We shall have to abide by our first decision," said Mrs. Morland. "By Mrs. Watkinson, mentioning in her note the hour of nine, it is to be presumed she intends asking some other company. I cannot possibly disappoint her. I can speak feelingly as to the annoyance (for I have known it by my own experience) when after inviting a number of my friends to meet some strangers, the strangers have sent an excuse almost at the eleventh hour. I think no inducements, however strong, could tempt me to do so myself."

"I confess that you are perfectly right," said Mrs. St. Leonard. "I see you must go to Mrs. Watkinson. But can you not divide the evening, by passing a part of it with her and then finishing with me?"

At this suggestion the eyes of the young people sparkled, for they had become delighted with Mrs. St. Leonard, and imagined that a party at her house must be every way charming. Also, parties were novelties to both of them.

"If possible we will do so," answered Mrs. Morland, "and with what pleasure I need not assure you. We leave New York to-morrow, but we shall return this way in September, and will then be exceedingly happy to see more of Mrs. St. Leonard."

After a little more conversation Mrs. St. Leonard took her leave, repeating her hope of still seeing her new friends at her house that night; and enjoining them to let her know as soon as they returned to New York on their way home.

Edward Morland handed her to her carriage, and then joined his mother and sister in their commendations of Mrs. St. Leonard, with whose exceeding beauty were united a countenance beaming with intelligence, and a manner that put every one at their ease immediately.

"She is an evidence," said Edward, "how superior our women of fashion are to those of Europe."

"Wait, my dear son," said Mrs. Morland, "till you have been in Europe, and had an opportunity of forming an opinion on that point (as on many others) from actual observation. For my part, I believe that in all civilized countries the upper classes of people are very much alike, at least in their leading characteristics."

"Ah! here comes the man that was sent to Mrs. Watkinson," said Caroline Morland. "I hope he could not find the house and has brought the note back with him. We shall then be able to go at first to Mrs. St. Leonard's, and pass the whole evening there."

The man reported that he *had* found the house, and had delivered the note into Mrs. Watkinson's own hands, as she chanced to be crossing the entry when the door was opened; and that she read it immediately, and said "Very well."

"Are you certain that you made no mistake in the house," said Edward, "and that you really *did* give it to Mrs. Watkinson?"

"And it's quite sure I am, sir," replied the man, "when I first came over from the ould country I lived with them awhile, and though when she saw me to-day, she did not let on that she remembered my doing that same, she could not help calling me James. Yes, the rale words she said when I handed her the billy-dux was, 'Very well, James.'"

"Come, come," said Edward, when they found themselves alone, "let us look on the bright side. If we do not find a large party at Mrs. Watkinson's, we may in all probability meet some very agreeable people there, and enjoy the feast of reason and the flow of soul. We may find the Watkinson house so pleasant as to leave it with regret even for Mrs. St. Leonard's."

"I do not believe Mrs. Watkinson is in fashionable society," said Caroline, "or Mrs. St. Leonard would have known her. I heard some of the ladies here talking last evening of Mrs. St. Leonard, and I found from what they said that she is among the *élite* of the *lite*."

"Even if she is," observed Mrs. Morland, "are polish of manners and cultivation of mind confined exclusively to persons of that class?"

"Certainly not," said Edward, "the most talented and refined youth at our college, and he in whose society I found the greatest pleasure, was the son of a bricklayer."

In the ladies' drawing-room, after dinner, the Morlands heard a conversation between several of the female guests, who all seemed to know Mrs. St. Leonard very well by reputation, and they talked of her party that was to "come off" on this evening.

"I hear," said one lady, "that Mrs. St. Leonard is to have an unusual number of lions."

She then proceeded to name a gallant general, with his elegant wife and accomplished daughter; a celebrated commander in the navy; two highly distinguished members of Congress, and even an ex-president. Also several of the most eminent among the American literati, and two first-rate artists.

Edward Morland felt as if he could say, "Had I three ears I'd hear thee."

"Such a woman as Mrs. St. Leonard can always command the best lions that are to be found," observed another lady.

"And then," said a third, "I have been told that she has such exquisite taste in lighting and embellishing her always elegant rooms. And her supper table, whether for summer or winter parties, is so beautifully arranged; all the viands are so delicious, and the attendance of the servants so perfect—and Mrs. St. Leonard does the honors with so much ease and tact."

"Some friends of mine that visit her," said a fourth lady, "describe her parties as absolute perfection. She always manages to bring together those persons that are best fitted to enjoy each other's conversation. Still no one is overlooked or neglected. Then everything at her reunions is so well proportioned—she has just enough of music, and just enough of whatever amusement may add to the pleasure of her guests; and still there is no appearance of design or management on her part."

"And better than all," said the lady who had spoken first; "Mrs. St. Leonard is one of the kindest, most generous, and most benevolent of women—she does good in every possible way."

"I can listen no longer," said Caroline to Edward, rising to change her seat. "If I hear any more I shall

14

absolutely hate the Watkinsons. How provoking that they should have sent us the first invitation. If we had only thought of waiting till we could hear from Mrs. St. Leonard!"

"For shame, Caroline," said her brother, "how can you talk so of persons you have never seen, and to whom you ought to feel grateful for the kindness of their invitation; even if it has interfered with another party, that I must confess seems to offer unusual attractions. Now I have a presentiment that we shall find the Watkinson part of the evening very enjoyable."

As soon as tea was over, Mrs. Morland and her daughter repaired to their toilettes. Fortunately, fashion as well as good taste, has decided that, at a summer party, the costume of the ladies should never go beyond an elegant simplicity. Therefore our two ladies in preparing for their intended appearance at Mrs. St. Leonard's, were enabled to attire themselves in a manner that would not seem out of place in the smaller company they expected to meet at the Watkinsons. Over an under-dress of lawn, Caroline Morland put on a white organdy trimmed with lace, and decorated with bows of pink ribbon. At the back of her head was a wreath of fresh and beautiful pink flowers, tied with a similar ribbon. Mrs. Morland wore a black grenadine over a satin, and a lace cap trimmed with white.

It was but a quarter past nine o'clock when their carriage stopped at the Watkinson door. The front of the house looked very dark. Not a ray gleamed through the Venetian shutters, and the glimmer beyond the fan-light over the door was almost imperceptible. After the coachman had rung several times, an Irish girl opened the door, cautiously (as Irish girls always do), and admitted them into the entry, where one light only was burning in a branch lamp. "Shall we go upstairs?" said Mrs. Morland. "And what for would ye go upstairs?" said the girl in a pert tone. "It's all dark there, and there's no preparations. Ye can lave your things here a-hanging on the rack. It is a party ye're expecting? Blessed are them what expects nothing."

The sanguine Edward Morland looked rather blank at this intelligence, and his sister whispered to him, "We'll get off to Mrs. St. Leonard's as soon as we possibly can. When did you tell the coachman to come for us?"

"At half past ten," was the brother's reply.

"Oh! Edward, Edward!" she exclaimed, "And I dare say he will not be punctual. He may keep us here till eleven."

"*Courage, mes enfants,*" said their mother, "*et parlez plus doucement.*"

The girl then ushered them into the back parlor, saying, "Here's the company."

The room was large and gloomy. A checquered mat covered the floor, and all the furniture was encased in striped calico covers, and the lamps, mirrors, etc. concealed under green gauze. The front parlor was entirely dark, and in the back apartment was no other light than a shaded lamp on a large centre table, round which was assembled a circle of children of all sizes and ages. On a backless, cushionless sofa sat Mrs. Watkinson, and a young lady, whom she introduced as her daughter Jane. And Mrs. Morland in return presented Edward and Caroline.

"Will you take the rocking-chair, ma'am?" inquired Mrs. Watkinson.

Mrs. Morland declining the offer, the hostess took it herself, and see-sawed on it nearly the whole time. It was a very awkward, high-legged, crouch-backed rocking-chair, and shamefully unprovided with anything in the form of a footstool.

"My husband is away, at Boston, on business," said Mrs. Watkinson. "I thought at first, ma'am, I should not be able to ask you here this evening, for it is not our way to have company in his absence; but my daughter Jane over-persuaded me to send for you."

"What a pity," thought Caroline.

"You must take us as you find us, ma'am," continued Mrs. Watkinson. "We use no ceremony with anybody; and our rule is never to put ourselves out of the way. We do not give parties [looking at the dresses of the ladies]. Our first duty is to our children, and we cannot waste our substance on fashion and folly. They'll have cause to thank us for it when we die."

Something like a sob was heard from the centre table, at which the children were sitting, and a boy was seen to hold his handkerchief to his face.

"Joseph, my child," said his mother, "do not cry. You have no idea, ma'am, what an extraordinary boy that is. You see how the bare mention of such a thing as our deaths has overcome him."

There was another sob behind the handkerchief, and the Morlands thought it now sounded very much like a smothered laugh.

"As I was saying, ma'am," continued Mrs. Watkinson, "we never give parties. We leave all sinful things to the vain and foolish. My daughter Jane has been telling me, that she heard this morning of a party that is going on tonight at the widow St. Leonard's. It is only fifteen years since her husband died. He was carried off with a three days' illness, but two months after they were married. I have had a domestic that lived with them at the time, so I know all about it. And there she is now, living in an elegant house, and riding in her carriage, and dressing and dashing, and giving parties, and enjoying life, as she calls it. Poor creature, how I pity her! Thank heaven, nobody that I know goes to her parties. If they did I would never wish to see them again in my house. It is an encouragement to folly and nonsense—and folly

19

and nonsense are sinful. Do not you think so, ma'am?"

"If carried too far they may certainly become so," replied Mrs. Morland.

"We have heard," said Edward, "that Mrs. St. Leonard, though one of the ornaments of the gay world, has a kind heart, a beneficent spirit and a liberal hand."

"I know very little about her," replied Mrs. Watkinson, drawing up her head, "and I have not the least desire to know any more. It is well she has no children; they'd be lost sheep if brought up in her fold. For my part, ma'am," she continued, turning to Mrs. Morland, "I am quite satisfied with the quiet joys of a happy home. And no mother has the least business with any other pleasures. My innocent babes know nothing about plays, and balls, and parties; and they never shall. Do they look as if they had been accustomed to a life of pleasure?"

They certainly did not! for when the Morlands took a glance at them, they thought they had never seen youthful faces that were less gay, and indeed less prepossessing.

There was not a good feature or a pleasant expression among them all. Edward Morland recollected his having often read "that childhood is always lovely." But he saw that the juvenile Watkinsons were an exception to the rule.

"The first duty of a mother is to her children," repeated Mrs. Watkinson. "Till nine o'clock, my daughter Jane and myself are occupied every evening in hearing the lessons that they have learned for to-morrow's school. Before that hour we can receive no visitors, and we never have company to tea, as that would interfere too much with our duties. We had just finished hearing these lessons when you arrived. Afterwards the children are permitted to indulge themselves in rational play, for I permit no amusement that is not also instructive. My children are so well trained, that even when alone their sports are always serious."

Two of the boys glanced slyly at each other, with what Edward Morland comprehended as an expression of pitch-penny and marbles.

"They are now engaged at their game of astronomy," continued Mrs. Watkinson. "They have also a sort of geography cards, and a set of mathematical cards. It is a blessed discovery, the invention of these educationary games; so that even the play-time of children can be turned to account. And you have no idea, ma'am, how they enjoy them."

Just then the boy Joseph rose from the table, and stalking up to Mrs. Watkinson, said to her, "Mamma, please to whip me."

At this unusual request the visitors looked much amazed, and Mrs. Watkinson replied to him, "Whip you, my best Joseph—for what cause? I have not seen you do anything wrong this evening, and you know my anxiety induces me to watch my children all the time."

"You could not see me," answered Joseph, "for I have not *done* anything very wrong. But I have had a bad thought, and you know Mr. Ironrule says that a fault imagined is just as wicked as a fault committed."

"You see, ma'am, what a good memory he has," said Mrs. Watkinson aside to Mrs. Morland. "But my best Joseph, you make your mother tremble. What fault have you imagined? What was your bad thought?"

"Ay," said another boy, "what's your thought like?"

"My thought," said Joseph, "was 'Confound all astronomy, and I could see the man hanged that made this game.'"

"Oh! my child," exclaimed the mother, stopping her ears, "I am indeed shocked. I am glad you repented so immediately."

"Yes," returned Joseph, "but I am afraid my repentance won't last. If I am not whipped, I may have these bad thoughts whenever I play at astronomy, and worse still at the geography game. Whip me, ma, and punish me as I deserve. There's the rattan in the corner: I'll bring it to you myself."

"Excellent boy!" said his mother. "You know I always pardon my children when they are so candid as to confess their faults."

"So you do," said Joseph, "but a whipping will cure me better."

"I cannot resolve to punish so conscientious a child," said   Mrs. Watkinson.

"Shall I take the trouble off your hands?" inquired Edward, losing all patience in his disgust at the sanctimonious hypocrisy of this young Blifil. "It is such a rarity for a boy to request a whipping, that so remarkable a desire ought by all means to be gratified."

Joseph turned round and made a face at him.

"Give me the rattan," said Edward, half laughing, and offering to take it out of his hand. "I'll use it to your full satisfaction."

The boy thought it most prudent to stride off and return to the table, and ensconce himself among his brothers and sisters; some of whom were staring with stupid surprise; others were whispering and giggling in the hope of seeing Joseph get a real flogging.

Mrs. Watkinson having bestowed a bitter look on Edward, hastened to turn the attention of his mother to something else. "Mrs. Morland," said she, "allow me to introduce you to my youngest hope." She pointed to a sleepy boy about five years old, who with head thrown back and mouth wide open, was slumbering in his chair.

Mrs. Watkinson's children were of that uncomfortable species who never go to bed; at least never without all manner of resistance. All her boasted authority was inadequate to compel them; they never would confess themselves sleepy; always wanted to "sit up," and there was a nightly scene of scolding, coaxing, threatening and manoeuvring to get them off.

"I declare," said Mrs. Watkinson, "dear Benny is almost asleep. Shake him up, Christopher. I want him to speak a speech. His school-mistress takes great pains in teaching her little pupils to speak, and stands up herself and shows them how."

The child having been shaken up hard (two or three others helping Christopher), rubbed his eyes and began to whine. His mother went to him, took him on her lap, hushed him up, and began to coax him.

This done, she stood him on his feet before Mrs. Morland, and desired him to speak a speech for the company. The child put his thumb into his mouth, and remained silent.

"Ma," said Jane Watkinson, "you had better tell him what speech to speak."

"Speak Cato or Plato," said his mother. "Which do you call it? Come now, Benny—how does it begin? 'You are quite right and reasonable, Plato.' That's it."

"Speak Lucius," said his sister Jane. "Come now, Benny—say 'your thoughts are turned on peace.'"

The little boy looked very much as if they were *not*, and as if meditating an outbreak.

"No, no!" exclaimed Christopher, "let him say Hamlet. Come now, Benny—'To be or not to be.'"

"It ain't to be at all," cried Benny, "and I won't speak the least bit of it for any of you. I hate that speech!"

"Only see his obstinacy," said the solemn Joseph. "And is he to be given up to?"

"Speak anything, Benny," said Mrs. Watkinson, "anything so that it is only a speech."

All the Watkinson voices now began to clamor violently at the obstinate child—"Speak a speech! speak a speech! speak a speech!" But they had no more effect than the reiterated exhortations with which nurses confuse the poor heads of babies, when they require them to "shake a day-day—shake a day-day!"

Mrs. Morland now interfered, and begged that the sleepy little boy might be excused; on which he screamed out that "he wasn't sleepy at all, and would not go to bed ever."

"I never knew any of my children behave so before," said Mrs. Watkinson. "They are always models of obedience, ma'am. A look is sufficient for them. And I must say that they have in every way profited by the education we are giving them. It is not our way, ma'am, to waste our money in parties and fooleries, and fine furniture and fine clothes, and rich food, and all such abominations. Our first duty is to our children, and to make them learn everything that is taught in the schools. If they go wrong, it will not be for want of education. Hester, my dear, come and talk to Miss Morland in French."

Hester (unlike her little brother that would not speak a speech) stepped boldly forward, and addressed Caroline Morland with: "*Parlez-vous Français, mademoiselle? Comment se va madame votre mère? Aimez-vous la musique? Aimez-vous la danse? Bon jour—bon soir—bon repos. Comprenez-vous?*"

To this tirade, uttered with great volubility, Miss Morland made no other reply than, "*Oui—je comprens.*"

"Very well, Hester—very well indeed," said Mrs. Watkinson. "You see, ma'am," turning to Mrs. Morland, "how very fluent she is in French; and she has only been learning eleven quarters."

After considerable whispering between Jane and her mother, the former withdrew, and sent in by the Irish girl a waiter with a basket of soda biscuit, a pitcher of water, and some glasses. Mrs. Watkinson invited her guests to consider themselves at home and help themselves freely, saying: "We never let cakes, sweetmeats, confectionery, or any such things enter the house, as they would be very unwholesome for the children, and it would be sinful to put temptation in their way. I am sure, ma'am, you will agree with me that the plainest food is the best for everybody. People that want nice things may go to parties for them; but they will never get any with me."

When the collation was over, and every child provided with a biscuit, Mrs. Watkinson said to Mrs. Morland: "Now, ma'am, you shall have some music from my daughter Jane, who is one of Mr. Bangwhanger's best scholars."

Jane Watkinson sat down to the piano and commenced a powerful piece of six mortal pages, which she played out of time and out of tune; but with tremendous force of hands; notwithstanding which, it had, however, the good effect of putting most of the children to sleep.

To the Morlands the evening had seemed already five hours long. Still it was only half past ten when Jane was in the midst of her piece. The guests had all tacitly determined that it would be best not to let Mrs. Watkinson know their intention to go directly from her house to Mrs. St. Leonard's party; and the arrival of their carriage would have been the signal of departure, even if Jane's piece had not reached its termination. They stole glances at the clock on the mantel. It wanted but a quarter of eleven, when Jane rose from the piano, and was congratulated by her mother on the excellence of her music. Still no carriage was heard to stop; no doorbell was heard to ring. Mrs. Morland expressed her fears that the coachman had forgotten to come for them.

"Has he been paid for bringing you here?" asked Mrs. Watkinson.

"I paid him when we came to the door," said Edward. "I thought perhaps he might want the money for some purpose before he came for us."

"That was very kind in you, sir," said Mrs. Watkinson, "but not very wise. There's no dependence on any coachman; and perhaps as he may be sure of business enough this rainy night he may never come at all—being already paid for bringing you here."

Now, the truth was that the coachman *had* come at the appointed time, but the noise of Jane's piano had prevented his arrival being heard in the back parlor. The Irish girl had gone to the door when he rang the bell, and recognized in him what she called "an ould friend." Just then a lady and gentleman who had been caught in the rain came running along, and seeing a carriage drawing up at a door, the gentleman inquired of the driver if he could not take them to Rutgers Place. The driver replied that he had just come for two ladies and a gentleman whom he had brought from the Astor House.

"Indeed and Patrick," said the girl who stood at the door, "if I was you I'd be after making another penny to-night. Miss Jane is pounding away at one of her long music pieces, and it won't be over before you have time to get to Rutgers and back again. And if you do make them wait awhile, where's the harm? They've a dry roof over their heads, and I warrant it's not the first waiting they've ever had in their lives; and it won't be the last neither."

"Exactly so," said the gentleman; and regardless of the propriety of first sending to consult the persons who had engaged the carriage, he told his wife to step in, and following her instantly himself, they drove away to Rutgers Place.

Reader, if you were ever detained in a strange house by the non-arrival of your carriage, you will easily understand the excessive annoyance of finding that you are keeping a family out of their beds beyond their usual hour. And in this case, there was a double grievance; the guests being all impatience to get off to a better place. The children, all crying when wakened from their sleep, were finally taken to bed by two servant maids, and Jane Watkinson, who never came back again. None were left but Hester, the great French scholar, who, being one of those young imps that seem to have the faculty of living without sleep, sat bolt upright with her eyes wide open, watching the uncomfortable visitors.

The Morlands felt as if they could bear it no longer, and Edward proposed sending for another carriage to the nearest livery stable.

"We don't keep a man now," said Mrs. Watkinson, who sat nodding in the rocking-chair, attempting now and then a snatch of conversation, and saying "ma'am" still more frequently than usual. "Men servants are dreadful trials, ma'am, and we gave them up three years ago. And I don't know how Mary or Katy are to go out this stormy night in search of a livery stable."

"On no consideration could I allow the women to do so," replied Edward. "If you will oblige me by the loan of an umbrella, I will go myself."

Accordingly he set out on this business, but was unsuccessful at two livery stables, the carriages being all out. At last he found one, and was driven in it to Mr. Watkinson's house, where his mother and sister were awaiting him, all quite ready, with their calashes and shawls on. They gladly took their leave; Mrs. Watkinson rousing herself to hope they had spent a pleasant evening, and that they would come and pass another with her on their return to New York. In such cases how difficult it is to reply even with what are called "words of course."

A kitchen lamp was brought to light them to the door, the entry lamp having long since been extinguished. Fortunately the rain had ceased; the stars began to reappear, and the Morlands, when they found themselves in the carriage and on their way to Mrs. St. Leonard's, felt as if they could breathe again. As may be supposed, they freely discussed the annoyances of the evening; but now those troubles were over they felt rather inclined to be merry about them.

"Dear mother," said Edward, "how I pitied you for having to endure Mrs. Watkinson's perpetual 'ma'aming' and 'ma'aming'; for I know you dislike the word."

"I wish," said Caroline, "I was not so prone to be taken with ridiculous recollections. But really to-night I could not get that old foolish child's play out of my head—

　Here come three knights out of Spain
　A-courting of your daughter Jane."

"I shall certainly never be one of those Spanish knights," said Edward. "Her daughter Jane is in no danger of being ruled by any 'flattering tongue' of mine. But what a shame for us to be talking of them in this manner."

They drove to Mrs. St. Leonard's, hoping to be yet in time to pass half an hour there; though it was now near twelve o'clock and summer parties never continue to a very late hour. But as they came into the street in which she lived they were met by a number of coaches on their way home, and on reaching the door of her brilliantly lighted mansion, they saw the last of the guests driving off in the last of the carriages, and several musicians coming down the steps with their instruments in their hands.

"So there *has* been a dance, then!" sighed Caroline. "Oh, what we have missed! It is really too provoking."

"So it is," said Edward; "but remember that to-morrow morning we set off for Niagara."

"I will leave a note for Mrs. St. Leonard," said his mother, "explaining that we were detained at Mrs. Watkinson's by our coachman disappointing us. Let us console ourselves with the hope of seeing more of this lady on our return. And now, dear Caroline, you must draw a moral from the untoward events of to-day. When you are mistress of a house, and wish to show civility to strangers, let the invitation be always accompanied with a frank disclosure of what they are to expect. And if you cannot conveniently invite company to meet them, tell them at once that you will not insist on their keeping their engagement with *you* if anything offers afterwards that they think they would prefer; provided only that they apprize you in time of the change in their plan."

"Oh, mamma," replied Caroline, "you may be sure I shall always take care not to betray my visitors into an engagement which they may have cause to regret, particularly if they are strangers whose time is limited. I shall certainly, as you say, tell them not to consider themselves bound to me if they afterwards receive an invitation which promises them more enjoyment. It will be a long while before I forget, the Watkinson evening."

End of the book.

www.ingramcontent.com/pod-product-compliance
Lightning Source LLC
Chambersburg PA
CBHW060016300526
45794CB00003B/1197